e|Merg   0

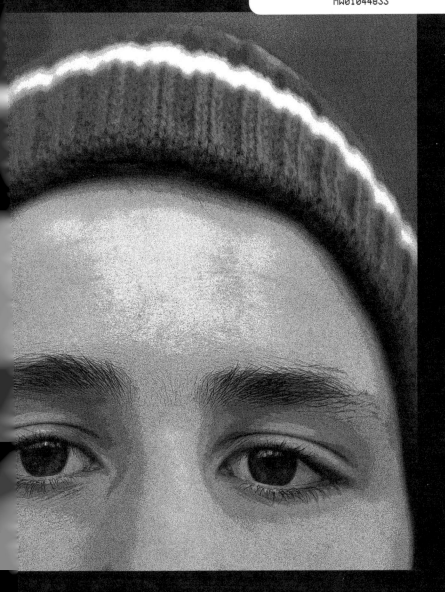

Developing Youth as Fully Devoted Disciples

mall-Group Leader's Guide for
Older Youth

07   08   09   10   11   12   13   14   15   16—10   9   8   7   6   5   4   3   2   1

Cover Design: Keely Moore

Contents

How to Use This Resource

Congratulations on being called to minister to youth as a small-group leader! As a small-group leader, you will work with students in an intimate setting, taking what the youth have learned from the large-group teaching sessions and going deeper through activities, discussion, and Bible study.

This book (and accompanying CD-ROM) gives you lesson plans, handouts, key Scriptures, and discussion questions for thirteen 45-minute sessions with your small group. You'll find at the beginning of each session plan "The Big Idea" (the key teaching for that session), "Session Texts" (the key Scriptures for that session), and "Before You Teach This Lesson," (personal reflection as you prepare for the session).

Each lesson plan then includes the following:

• **Warm-up:** an opening game related to the key teaching for the session.

• **Teaching:** a summary of what youth should learn from that session and why it is important.

• **Handout:** a worksheet that the youth complete individually or in small groups that will get them thinking about the key teaching for that session and how it applies to their lives. Printable PDFs of these handouts are found on the CD-ROM. Information for discussing each question on each handout is provided in this book.

• **Look at the Book:** a short Bible study that explores the key Scriptures for that session.

• **Wrap-up:** a summary of what the youth should take away from the session, and a suggestion for a closing prayer.

The CD-ROM also includes three audio tracks that help you better understand your role as a small-group leader and give you tips on how to best serve the youth in your small group. You can listen to these tracks with a CD or MP3 player.

How to Use the CD-ROM: To listen to the audio tracks, place the CD-ROM in a standard audio CD player. To access the printable handouts or to download MP3 files of the audio tracks, insert the CD-ROM into your computer.

Glow: Hanging Out With God

The Big Idea

Youth need to find a time and a place in which they can "get real" with God. When they consistently hang out with God, they will glow with the Holy Spirit; God's heart will become their heart, and they will receive God's wisdom.

Session Texts

• **Exodus 34:33-35** (Moses comes down from the mountain.)

• **Mark 1:35** (Jesus goes to a deserted place to spend time with God.)

Before You Teach This Lesson

We cannot expect to take students to a place where we have not been ourselves. All leadership begins with self-leadership. Are you creating space in your life for God to speak to you? Do you model the importance of time with God on a daily basis?

Think through these questions to prepare for teaching this lesson:

• How much ease do you have making time for God every day? What makes it difficult? What makes it easy?

• Can you describe in one sentence why time with God should be a priority for teenagers?

Opener: Blind Spot

> **What You'll Need**
> pen and half a sheet of paper for each youth

Have each student draw, on the left side of the sheet, a circle the size of a dime. Ask the youth to fill in the circle. On the right side of the page, about five inches from the circle, have each student draw an X that is about the same size as the circle.

Instruct the youth to close their right eye and focus their left eye on the X. Have them hold their paper about ten inches from their face. Even though they are focusing on the X, they should be able to see the circle out of the corner of their eye. Instruct the youth to move their papers from the left to the right, toward their face and back out. At some point, the circle will disappear into a blind spot.

Say, "When the circle falls into your blind spot, you can't see it even though you know it's there." Then ask:

- What do you know about blind spots? In what other situations have you heard that phrase? *(Youth who drive, for example, will know that drivers should check their blind spots before changing lanes.)*

- Has anything happened in your life that you didn't notice even though it was right in front of your face?

- What are some common "blind spots" that many teens choose to ignore even though these problems might be obvious to others?

Teaching

Often the habits that one develops during the later teenage years carry over into adulthood. If our high school youth are to become adults who spend time daily with God, now is the time to establish these habits.

What You'll Need
copies of "Hanging Out With God" worksheet (on the CD-ROM)

Handout: Hanging Out With God

Hand out copies of "Hanging Out With God," and have the youth to complete it in pairs or groups of three.

Then discuss the handout, using these discussion points:

1. Tell the youth that one common reason cited for not spending time with God is simply not having enough time. Have the students calculate the total number of hours they spend on the activities listed in the upper half of the page. Instruct them to subtract this total from 168, the total number of hours in a week. How much time is left? If a youth doesn't have much time left, ask him or her to think about what he or she could eliminate.

2. Discuss what factors make the students feel close to God.

3. Invite the students to talk about what areas of their lives need the Lord's guidance, but do not pressure anyone to speak up.

4. Discuss how time with God affects our feelings, attitudes, and perspective on life.

Look at the Book

Invite one student to read aloud **Exodus 34:33-35.**

Say: "After spending time alone with God, Moses glowed so brightly that he had to wear a veil. Everyone who saw him could tell that he had been in the presence of the Lord."

Ask:

• How can people tell that you've made a habit of spending time with God in prayer or devotion?

• Whom do you know who "glows" because they have such a strong relationship with God? How do their words and actions demonstrate their love for God?

Ask another youth to read aloud **Mark 1:35.**

Say: "Jesus, even though he was one with God, made spending time alone with his heavenly Father a priority."

Ask:

• Why, do you think, did Jesus—the Messiah and God in human form—felt the need to spend time alone in prayer?

• How do you feel after spending time alone with God?

Wrap-up

Instruct each person to write down a time and place when and where he or she can spend time with God each day. Encourage the students to use this time for prayer, devotion, and Scripture reading; and tell them that you'll check up on their progress.

E-mail, text message, call, or instant message your youth during the week to see how they're doing.

Close in prayer, thanking God for loving to spend time with us.

Glow: Prayer

The Big Idea

Prayer is simply a conversation with God. The elegance of our words doesn't matter as much as our attitude and the orientation of our hearts. Prayer is as much about listening to God as it is talking to God. Jesus gave us an example of how to pray: the Lord's Prayer.

Session Text

• **Matthew 6:6** (Jesus instructs his followers to find a quiet, secluded place to pray.)

• **Matthew 6:9-13** (the Lord's Prayer)

Before You Teach This Lesson

In the Christian faith, prayer is all around us. Many church meetings begin with prayer, as we ask God to guide our decisions. Most services include corporate prayers. But congregational worship should never be a substitute for personal prayer. God desires to hear from us in a personal and intimate way. Prayer realigns our focus from ourselves to God.

How is your prayer life? Reflect on these questions:

• How intimate is your prayer life? How often do you spend time alone with God?

• How fresh is your prayer life? Do your prayers ever seem stale or recycled? How do you keep your prayers fresh?

• How effectively do you focus on God during your prayers? Do you often find your mind wandering?

• How balanced are your prayers? Do you have a conversation with God in which you actively listen, or do you do all the talking?

• If you had one hour to communicate biblical and theological truth about prayer to your students, what would you say and do?

Discussion

Here are some questions to get your group thinking about prayer:

• If someone asked you, "What is prayer?" how would you answer?

• What would you say to a three-year-old who wanted to learn to pray?

• How did you learn to pray? Who were your teachers?

Teaching

Prayer, a vital part of Christian life, is simply talking and listening to God. We need to communicate with God much like we need to communicate with a close friend or a parent. If you were to go a long time without talking to such a person, you would fall out of touch with him or her. Likewise, if we don't regularly go to God in prayer, we will be out of touch with what the Lord is asking us to do.

Handout: Prayer Philosophy

Distribute copies of the "Prayer Philosophy" handout, and instruct the youth to complete it in pairs or groups of three. Discuss their answers, using the discussion points below.

> **What You'll Need**
> copies of "Prayer Philosophy" worksheet (on the CD-ROM)

1–2. Invite the youth to read their answers for these questions. Ask:

• How important should prayer be in a Christian's life?

• How would your everyday life be different if you spent more time in prayer? if you didn't pray?

3. Discuss each statement, mentioning how you responded to each one.

4. Invite the youth to read aloud their summaries of what the listed Scriptures say about prayer. Then challenge the youth to think of how each of the Scriptures applies to their personal prayer lives.

What You'll Need

copies of "How to Pray"
worksheet (on the CD-ROM),
dictionaries and thesauruses
(optional)

Look at the Book

Hand out copies of the "How to Pray" worksheet, and instruct the youth to read through the Lord's Prayer as it is printed on the handout. Then give the students plenty of time to rewrite the prayer in their own words. When most of the youth have finished, invite volunteers to read aloud their versions of the Lord's Prayer.

Wrap-up

God is eager to talk to us every day. When we pray, we should focus on being honest with God and listening as God speaks to us. Encourage your youth to pray this week by using one or more of the following methods:

• Write your prayer in the form of a letter to God.

• Find a space where you can comfortably pray aloud to God.

• Pray Scripture. Many of the psalms make excellent prayers.

• Carve out five minutes each day when you can be completely silent and allow yourself to focus on what God is saying to you.

• Pray with a group of friends, giving each one a chance to pray aloud.

• Pray for individual people you know by name. For each person, think of one word that describes how you would like them to experience God's presence (such as *healing, strength,* and *guidance*).

• Keep a prayer journal. Record concerns, praises, and other prayer requests. Include the dates of when you added each prayer requests and update the journal so that you can keep track of how God is answering your prayers.

Glow: The Word

The Big Idea

God's Word is more than a collection of stories; it shows the Lord's interaction with God's people over time. This story continues and offers guidance for living, as well as transformation.

Session Texts

• **Psalm 119:9** (How young people can keep their way pure)

• **Proverbs 30:5-6** (Trusting in God, not relying on one's own insight)

• **Matthew 7:24-27** (The wise man and the foolish man)

• **2 Timothy 3:14-17** (Scripture: inspired by God and useful)

• **Hebrews 4:12** (The living and active Word of God)

• **James 1:22** (Being doers of the Word, not just hearers)

Before You Teach This Lesson

What are your views on reading the Bible? How is it exciting? When is it tedious? What do you think is the best setting for reading Scripture?

Perhaps you heard Bible stories while growing up. These stories can become a part of the fabric of our faith and stick with us throughout our lives. As we mature, the Holy Spirit uses the texts that we learned as children to light our paths. Paul tells us that "all Scripture is inspired by God and is useful for teaching, for reproof, for correction, and for training in righteousness" (**2 Timothy 3:16**).

Think through these questions as you prepare to teach this session:

• Aside from when you are preparing a lesson or talk or writing something for church, how often do you read the Bible?

• What has the Holy Spirit revealed to you recently through Scripture?

• How has maturity changed how you view and interact with the Bible—mentally and spiritually?

• If you had only one hour to express to your students the importance of regular Scripture reading, what would you say?

Discussion

• What are your earliest memories of learning about the Bible?

• What are your favorite Bible stories?

• Why is the Bible important for our lives?

• What percent of people your age, do you think, read the Bible once a week? *(According to the National Study of Youth and Religion, only 32 percent of churchgoing teens read the Bible alone once a week or more.)*

• Have you discussed the Bible with your friends and peers? When have you had to defend the Bible as God's Word?

Teach

Over thousands of years the Bible has not changed. In less than six years, by contrast, Apple® has released five generations of the iPod. The Bible is not a stale relic, like dinosaur bones in a museum, but rather a living text that empowers us to do God's work by showing truth, correcting our mistakes, and training us to live God's way.

What You'll Need
copies of Worksheet titled "By the Book" (CD-ROM)

Handout: By the Book

Distribute copies of the worksheet, and allow youth to work in groups or on their own to answer the questions listed.

A quick word of caution: The youth may ask some questions that you cannot answer. If you find yourself in this position, be honest about not knowing the answer and do your best to find an answer before the next week's session.

1. Invite, but do not pressure, the youth to talk about their answers. Allow the students to elaborate on why they read or don't read the Bible more regularly.

   If the students are hung up on the Bible being hard to understand, suggest that they try different versions by using an online resource such as *www.biblegateway.com* or *www.biblecrosswalk.com*.

2. Invite the students to read aloud the questions they've written down. You might record them on a markerboard or large sheet of paper. If multiple youth ask similar questions, discuss these questions.

3. Ask volunteers to read aloud their answers. Talk about how the Bible has done each of these things (teaching, reproof and correction, and training in righteousness) in your life and in your church. You might mention how a group in your congregation used certain Scriptures to study a difficult issue or how the Bible shed light on some area of your life that needed to change.

4. Read aloud each of the Scriptures listed. After you read each one, allow the youth to read their summaries of that verse.

Look at the Book

Read aloud each of the Scriptures from question 4 of the worksheet (**Psalm 119:97-99; Proverbs 30:5-6; Hebrews 4:12; James 1:21-25;** and **1 Peter 2:1-3**). After reading each one, ask the following questions:

• What one word or phrase from this Scripture stands out to you? Why? How does it help you better understand the Scripture?

• How does this verse apply specifically to you and your peers?

• What about this Scripture do you find most challenging?

Wrap-up

Hebrews 4:12 tells us that the Bible is a living and active source for understanding God. Challenge your students to spend time with God every day. Discuss how the youth can encourage one another and hold one another accountable in reading Scripture daily.

Spend some time expressing to your students the importance of the Bible in your life. How has reading the Bible benefited you? How have you applied Scripture to your everyday life?

Close by praying **Psalm 119:1-8** (and using *The Message* if you can). Pause between each phrase to allow the students to reflect on the Scripture.

Room Raiders: The Family Room

The Big Idea

Many factors contribute to family stress, but you are in a unique position to make your overall family vibe better.

Session Texts

• **1 Corinthians 13:4-8a** (Love is patient, love is kind.)

Before You Teach This Lesson

The family unit is the most basic structural element of our culture. Many adolescents' greatest strengths or shortcomings are tied directly or indirectly to family dynamics.

Important

This lesson may be difficult for youth whose families are abusive or marred by broken relationships. While talking about patience, forgiveness, and honesty as characteristics of a loving family is important, some youth may not be ready to be patient, forgiving, or honest toward their families. As you need to, explain that in some situations anger is a normal and healthy response.

Think through these questions as you prepare to teach this lesson:

• How would you describe your family from your growing-up years?

• What are your favorite memories of your family?

• Were you the oldest, youngest, middle, or only child? How, do you think, did this trait influence your perspective on and relationship with your family?

• If you could have changed one thing about your family, what would it have been?

• If you had only one hour to convey biblical truth about family life to your students, what would you say and do?

Warm-up

Invite the teens to create a symbol for each member of their family. These designs can be as simple or complex as the youth would like. (The Superman symbol would qualify as simple; the Presidential Seal, more complex.) Encourage the teens to think of symbols that get at the heart of who each family member is. Allow five minutes for drawing, and make your own design; then allow each person to present his or her work.

Say, "List on the back of your drawing those things that you like least about your family." Give the youth some time to write; then say: "Now list on the back of your drawing those things that you like most about your family." Give the youth some time to write; then allow them to name those things they like most about their families

Say: "No two families are alike, but the bond that holds any family together is love. Today, we're going to talk about what real love is and how we can show real love to our families."

Handout: Love Is Patient, Love Is Kind

Hand out copies of "Love Is Patient, Love Is Kind," and instruct the youth to complete it in pairs or groups of three. Give them plenty of time to work; then discuss their answers.

1. Invite the students to read aloud the words they chose to describe their family. Make note of those words that multiple people chose and words that are unique to one or two people. Point out to the youth that their families have plenty in common with other families and are not weird. Also mention that when taken together, all of the characteristics that describe their family make it unique.

2. Build on your discussion of question 1, talking about the similarities and differences among various families.

3. Invite volunteers to read aloud their paraphrases. Consider posting them somewhere in your church building or meeting space.

Look at the Book

Ask volunteers to read aloud **1 Corinthians 13,** each person reading one or two verses. Then say: "Paul tells us in **1 Corinthians 13** the characteristics of real love. Let's go through verses 4–8a together."

Love is patient.

• When do you get impatient with your family?

• In what situations can you show more patience with your family?

Love is kind.

• How does the way you treat your family compare with the way you treat your friends? How can you be more kind to your family?

Love is not envious or boastful or arrogant.

• How competitive is your family? When do you boast to your family? In what ways do you envy certain family members?

• How do you or can you support your family members and compliment them on what they do well?

[Love is not] rude.

• When are you rude to your parents? What about your siblings?

• How can you demonstrate that love is not rude by treating your family with respect and sensitivity?

[Love] does not insist on its own way.

• When do you get so wrapped up in the issues you're facing that you don't pay attention to your family's wants and needs?

• What can you do to be more considerate of your family's wants, needs, and feelings?

It is not irritable. (Also translated as "It is not easily angered.")

• What about your family makes you angry or irritable?

• What makes your family happier and more agreeable?

[Love is not] resentful (or, "It keeps no record of wrongs").

• What grudges do you hold toward your parents or siblings?

• For what do you need to forgive siblings or parents right now?

It does not rejoice in wrongdoings, but rejoices in the truth.

• How honest are you with your parents and siblings?

• When are you tempted to hide the truth or to stretch the truth?

• What is most difficult about being completely honest?

• What are the benefits of being honest in all situations?

It bears all things, believes all things, hopes all things, endures all things.

Say: "Every family has problems; every family struggles with anger and dishonesty and holding grudges. But loving families work through these tough times with patience and kindness."

Love never ends.

Say: "Real love doesn't give up—it never fails. Love can be sticky and difficult, but love can also outlast any problems that arise."

Wrap-up

Lead the students in a discussion about ways that they can show their love for their families in simple and practical ways.

Have students close their eyes while you slowly read aloud **1 Corinthians 13:4-8a** one more time. Tell the youth to think about specific ways that these words apply to their families.

Room Raiders: The Kitchen

The Big Idea

The "You are what you eat" cliché is true. The kitchen is where we go to fill our bodies with the food that gives us energy. Likewise, in our spiritual lives, we need energy for daily living. We get this energy by developing habits that bring us closer to God.

Session Texts

• **Hebrews 5:14** (Solid food is for the mature.)

Before You Teach This Lesson

Good leadership begins with self-leadership. We cannot, with integrity, challenge students to spend time with God each day unless we ourselves practice spiritual disciplines.

Think through these questions as you prepare to teach this lesson:

• How full is your spiritual gas tank? When (or how often) do you find yourself running low on spiritual fuel?

• What spiritual disciplines do you practice regularly? How do these practices give you fuel for daily living?

• Why is this commitment to spiritual disciplines important to the teens you lead?

• If you only had one hour to talk to teenagers about daily spiritual habits, what would you want to convey?

> **What You'll Need**
> boxes of macaroni and cheese, any other ingredients needed

Warm-up

One of the illustrations in the large-group teaching involves macaroni and cheese. Build on this metaphor by serving mac and cheese to your group. You could bring in a big casserole dish of macaroni and cheese beforehand or have your youth work together to make it as an opening activity. (The latter option would let your youth spend time in the kitchen, which is this session's theme.) If some of your youth are lactose intolerant, look for dairy-free recipes.

Enjoy the food together as you discuss these questions:

• During a typical week, how much time do you spend with God in prayer, worship, and Scripture reading?

• What spiritual disciplines help you develop as a Christian?

Teaching

The kitchen is where we prepare the food that feeds our bodies. This session focuses on the food that feeds our souls.

Many older youth have to make decisions about commitments. Youth who played several sports as children may have to choose one so that they can more fully devote themselves to training and conditioning. Joining a community orchestra may involve setting aside more time each day to practice an instrument.

Help your students make connection between the commitments they make to these activities to the commitment they make to God.

Handout: Good Grub

Hand out copies of "Good Grub," and instruct the youth to complete it in pairs or groups of three. Give them plenty of time to work; then discuss their answers by using these discussion points:

> **What You'll Need**
> copies of the "Good Grub" worksheet (CD-ROM)

1. Ask the youth to draw from their knowledge of food groups and nutrition. What types of food need to be a part of every meal? What types of food do we need once a day? What types of food should we try to eliminate from our diets?

   What is the spiritual equivalent of a well-balanced meal? What gives our soul the energy it needs to get through the day?

2. Ask the youth to talk about the benefits of healthy, satisfying snacks. What do they eat when they need a burst of energy between meals? What is the spiritual equivalent of such snacks?

3. Why are we humans attracted to some foods that we know aren't good for us? What is the spiritual equivalent of these foods?

4. Ask the youth if their moods change when they skip breakfast. How do they feel if they eat too much for lunch? Which foods give them a burst of energy? Which foods make them feel ill?

5. The answers will vary and will probably be given in hours, not days. Going an entire day without food is unhealthy and leaves us hungry. So does going an entire day without feeding ourselves spiritually. Youth who have had experiences such as the 30-Hour Famine will have a unique perspective on this question.

Look at the Book

Ask one student to read aloud **Hebrews 5:13-14.**

Ask:

• How have your eating habits changed as you've matured?

• How does this metaphor apply to faith? When are we spiritually mature enough to handle solid food?

Say, "This verse also talks about training and practicing."

Invite the youth to talk about things that they practice or train for, such as sports, music, dance, theater, and their studies. Ask the teens to talk about how their performance suffers if they go several days or weeks without practice. Besides formal practice, have the youth talk about other habits they develop that help them improve their skills (such as eating healthy or getting a good night's sleep).

Wrap-up

Emphasize the importance of conditioning ourselves by developing spiritual habits. Making time each day for prayer and Scripture reading may require us to re-order our priorities, but these practices will help us grow as Christians and face life's challenges.

Close in prayer, asking God for help in developing habits that will help your youth grow spiritually.

Room Raiders: The Bathroom

The Big Idea

Image is everything in our culture. Both guys and girls spend hours in the bathroom crafting the image that they will present to the world. At times, the beautiful person whom God has created is lost under layers of masks. God loves the person within and knows each of us intimately and personally.

Session Texts

• **Genesis 1:27** (God creates humankind in God's image.)

• **Genesis 2:7-8, 21-22, 25** (Adam and Eve are naked and unashamed.)

• **1 Peter 1:23** (We are born anew into imperishable bodies.)

Before You Teach This Lesson

Think through these questions as you prepare to teach this lesson:

• In high school, how concerned were you about your image?

• What "looks" did you go for when you were a teenager?

• Right now, how important is the image you project to others? What perspective have you gained since your teenage years?

• If you had only one hour to talk to your students about self-image, what are the most important points you'd want to convey?

Teaching

Adolescence is a difficult time of life for many reasons, but it is especially difficult where body image in concerned. Teens spend every day of their lives amid peers at various stages in physical, mental, and emotional development; and they are constantly bombarded with unrealistic and unhealthy images of the "perfect body." High school youth especially may obsess about losing weight or gaining muscle; and coaches, dances instructors, and other respected adults in the teens' lives may unintentionally encourage youth to stop eating, take unhealthy supplements, or work out incessantly.

Warm-up: In the Bathroom

What You'll Need
several items commonly found in a bathroom (at least one for each youth)

Set out several items commonly found in a bathroom (such as a toothbrush, make up, hairspray, and so on). Ask the youth to select from these items one item that they use often. Have each youth one at a time present his or her item and say why and how often he or she uses this item and what life would be like without it.

Ask:

• How does knowing that you were made in God's image affect how you get ready in the morning and what you think of yourself when you look in the mirror?

Handout: Freshening Up

What You'll Need
copies of the "Freshening Up" worksheet (CD-ROM)

Hand out copies of "Freshening Up," and instruct the youth to complete it individually. Give the youth plenty of time to work; then divide the youth into same-sex groups to discuss the handout using the discussion points below. You will need to enlist an adult volunteer of the opposite sex from yours to lead the group that is of that sex.

1. Invite youth to talk about how much they look like their mother or father. (This discussion will be especially interesting if the youth know one another's parents well.) Be sensitive to youth who have never known their biological parents.

2. Only discuss the students' answers to this question if your youth support and respect one another. Tell the youth that all people have things that they don't like about their bodies and that our culture's idea of the perfect body is dangerous and unrealistic.

3. Allow youth to be as open or as restrained as they are comfortable being. Which of these things do they think are reasonable? Which seem excessive or ridiculous?

4. Ask the youth to talk about what is unreasonable or unhealthy about our culture's image of the perfect body.

5. Answers to this question may involve being pressured to go to great lengths to lose weight or build muscle or getting so frustrated with one's body that depression and anxiety result.

6. Answers might include eating disorders, taking supplements for short-term gain that have negative long-term consequences, or low self-esteem that leads to depression and self-destructive behavior.

Look at the Book

Read aloud **Genesis 1:27.** Say: "Scripture tells us that God created us in God's image, loves us, and sees beauty in each one of us."

Ask one volunteer to read aloud **Genesis 2:7-8,** another to read aloud verses **21-22,** and another to read aloud **25.**

Say: "Many people feel shame about their bodies at one time or another. And most of us, at some point, have asked ourselves, *Am I normal?*"

Ask:

• How did the first humans' attitudes toward their bodies differ from modern-day attitudes toward the human body?

• How would you describe a normal human body? *(Since every person is unique, there is no such thing as normal.)*

• How are you unique physically, mentally, or spiritually?

Ask a volunteer to read aloud **1 Peter 1:23-25a.**

Say: "We need to know that God loves us and considers each one of us beautiful; but we also need to know that our human bodies are temporary and that Christ will one day turn our earthly bodies into glorious, eternal bodies."

Wrap-up

Once again, affirm to youth that they are God's beloved creations and that while they are all made in God's image, each of them is uniquely beautiful. Close in prayer, asking God to help you and your group more clearly see the beauty in each person.

Room Raiders: The Garage

The Big Idea

We need to take an honest look at the junk that tends to pile up in our lives, so that we may dispose of the sin that gets in the way of what God desires for us.

Session Texts

• **Deuteronomy 6:5** ("You shall love the LORD your God with your heart, and with all your soul, and with all your might.")

• **Ezekiel 11:19** ("I will give them one heart, and put a new spirit within them; I will remove the heart of stone from their flesh and give them a heart of flesh.")

Before You Teach This Lesson

Just as we all have garbage in our house, we all have junk that clutters our hearts, minds, and souls. While the junk in our homes may consume valuable space, our spiritual junk consumes valuable energy and time that could be used in service to God and others.

As you prepare to teach this session, think about the spiritual junk that clutters your life, including holding grudges and lacking discipline. How can you "clean up" this junk in your life? What are the benefits of cleaning up your spiritual junk?

Teaching

Most families have a room or a space full of junk. This place may be a garage, an attic, or a closet. While few people enjoy cleaning out these spaces, most of us feel better after getting rid of our junk. By cleaning out the junk, we make more space for important things and may uncover valuable items that we'd forgotten or presumed lost.

This session focuses on spiritual junk, particularly grudges and lack of discipline. These types of junk can consume valuable energy, wear us down, and cover up more appealing aspects of our personality. This session is all about getting youth to look at their junk and think of better ways to use their hearts, minds, and energy.

Warm-up: In the Garage

Beforehand, come up with a rule that determines what answers are acceptable. For instance, the rule might be two words that begin with the same letter, and acceptable answers would include a "broken bicycle," "recycling receptacle," and "weed whacker."

To begin this game, say, "I went out to my garage and found . . . ." Complete the sentence by naming a piece of junk that is commonly found in a garage and fits your rule. Do not tell the students your rule.

One at a time, have youth try to complete the sentence with an acceptable answer. If a student gives an incorrect answer, say, "You did not go out to my garage." Once everyone has had a turn, come back to the youth who gave incorrect answers. Continue playing until everyone catches on and gives a correct answer.Play this game again if time permits, this time letting a youth come up with the rule.

Then invite the youth to talk about where their families keep their junk. What are the benefits of cleaning out the junk in our homes?

Handout: Me and My Junk

Hand out copies of "Me and My Junk," and instruct the youth to complete the worksheet. Give the students plenty of time to work; then discuss their answers by using these discussion points:

> **What You'll Need**
> copies of the "Me and My Junk" worksheet (on the CD-ROM)

1. Invite the youth to talk about where they keep their junk and what types of junk they hold on to.

2. Some households cannot park their cars in the garage because the garage is full of junk. And some families could set up their old table-tennis equipment in their basement if they bothered to make room for it.

   Ask the youth to think about any "spiritual junk" that has cluttered their lives. How do these types of junk consume time and energy that could be put to better use?

3. Again, ask the youth to think about the examples of spiritual junk discussed with previous question. Talk about how these kinds of spiritual junk can overshadow or hide the blessings in our lives.

4. Answers may range from laziness to being sentimentally attached to something they don't need. Follow up by asking youth why getting rid of their spiritual junk difficult?

Look at the Book

Ask volunteers to read aloud various translations of **Deuteronomy 6:5.**

Say: "This verse is from a section of Scripture known as the *shema,* because it begins in verse 4 with the Hebrew word *shema*, meaning 'hear.' The ancient Israelites considered this Scripture to be important, as do Jews today, because it sums up the people's relationship with God. They are to love the Lord with their whole hearts and souls and with all their might."

Ask:

• What do you need to get rid of that keeps you from fully loving God with your whole heart and soul? *(Don't pressure the youth to answer this question aloud.)*

Say: "To obey God's command in this Scripture, we need to get rid of the junk in our lives. Cleaning out all of our spiritual junk can be difficult; but God vows to help us."

Ask a volunteer to read aloud **Ezekiel 11:19-20.**

Say: "If we let go of our junk, God will help us clean house and will give us a new heart."

Wrap-up

Give the youth time to silently reflect on the spiritual junk that they hold on to. Challenge them to think of one thing they can do in the coming week to clean out the junk in their life.

Close in prayer, asking God to help your students clean out their junk and to give them "new hearts."

Room Raiders: The Bedroom

The Big Idea

Integrity involves not only acting in a way that's consistent with your words and beliefs but also who you are when no one is looking. Maintaining our integrity is an important part of our identity as Christians.

Session Texts

• **Job 2:1-10** (Satan tests Job, and Job maintains his integrity.)

• **Proverbs 11:3** (*Message*): ("The integrity of the honest keeps them on track; the deviousness of crooks brings them to ruin.")

Before You Teach This Lesson

Youth are great judges of integrity. For some reason, teenagers can sniff out fakers like police dogs sniff out narcotics. If our actions are inconsistent with our words and beliefs, our youth will catch us and call us out. We need to set an example for the students we work with by maintaining our integrity even when doing so is difficult or uncomfortable. Jesus said that "a student is not above his teacher, but everyone who is fully trained will be like his teacher" (**Luke 6:40, NIV**). These words both encourage and haunt teachers, mentors, and student ministers.

Think through these questions as you prepare to teach this lesson:

• When you think of people of integrity, who comes to mind? What do you admire most about these people?

• When, if ever, have you been tempted to mislead or hide something from your youth? How did you deal with these temptations?

• What can you do to make your actions more consistent with what you say and what you believe?

• If you had to tell one story that illustrates what integrity means, what story would you tell?

• If you had only one hour to teach students the importance of integrity, what would you say?

Opener: Case Studies

Read each of the vignettes below. After each one, ask youth which of the two options will produce the best outcome.

AP Chemistry

Sandy decided to take AP Chemistry because she thought it would help her realize her dream of attending an Ivy League school. She now needs an *A* on the final exam so that her final grade will be a *B;* with a lower test score, she will finish the year with a *C* average. The night before the final exam, her grandmother is rushed to the hospital with a heart problem.

After spending a sleepless (and study-less) night at the hospital, Sandy's academic life flashes before her eyes when the exam hits her desk. She prays to God for a miracle then gets to work. While she is struggling through the exam, her teacher is called to the office. After telling the students to keep their eyes on their own papers, he leaves the room. Thirty seconds after the teacher leaves, the entire class starts swapping answers. Brian, the best student in the class, feels confident in his answers and is willing to give them out.

Sandy asks herself, Is this the miracle I've been praying for?

Should Sandy be honest, or should she cheat?

If you said, "Be honest": The next day, Sandy gets her test back with a big, fat *C-* written on it in red ink. She gets a *C* in AP chemistry and doesn't get accepted by the Ivy League school of her dreams.

If you said, "Cheat": Sandy feverishly changes answers and writes down all the formulas she has forgotten and can now answer most of the questions on her exam. She gets an *A* on the test. The following year, she gets an acceptance letter from the college of her dreams.

Locker Room

Zach and Sarah have been close friends since fifth grade, when Zach had a crush on Sarah. Now in high school, Sarah is dating Aaron, a guy who is on Zach's wrestling team. The other day, after practice, Aaron told everyone about his relationship with Sarah and went way beyond "kiss and tell."

Zach knows Sarah well enough to know that Aaron's stories aren't true. As the testosterone level goes up in the locker room, Zach's teammates start cheering on Aaron and giving him high-fives. But at least one member of the team doubts Aaron's story and looks at Zach as to say, "Is Aaron telling the truth, or is he making this all up?"

Should Zach can go along with Aaron's story, or should he defend his friend and show up his teammate?

If you said, "Lie": Zach goes along with the story and decides not to show up his teammate. At first, Sarah has no idea; but she eventually learns from other members of the team that Aaron has been saying things about her that aren't true. Sarah is angry that Zach didn't stand up for her, and her relationship with Zach sours.

If you said, "Defend Sarah": When the wrestling team learns that Aaron isn't the stud that he said he was, entire room erupts in laughs and jeers. Sarah eventually hears about Aaron's lies and learns that Zach stood up for her. Zach earns a reputation as a guy who can be trusted and who is willing to take a stand for what is right.

Follow-up Questions

- In one scenario, having integrity had negative consequences in the short term; in the other scenario, having integrity had positive consequences in the short term. Why doesn't doing the right thing always have the best short-term consequences?

- How hard is it to be a person of integrity when being honest isn't the popular thing to do?

- When in your life has being honest been most difficult?

- How do the possible outcomes of your actions affect whether you act with integrity?

Teaching

The right thing isn't always the easy thing. In fact, many times, doing what is right is hard and the short-term consequences are even harder. But integrity isn't about immediate benefits; it's about growing in our relationships with God and others.

Youth need to be aware of how integrity affects relationships in the long term. If they act with integrity, even if the short-term consequences are negative, over time they will build trust and respect with their friends, families, and communities. If they do not, that trust and respect will erode over time, even if they see quick, positive results. In the end, the benefits of following God and maintaining one's integrity far outweigh the drawbacks.

> **What You'll Need**
> copies of the "Integrity" worksheet (on the CD-ROM)

Handout: Integrity

Hand out copies of the "Integrity" worksheet, and instruct the youth to complete it in pairs or groups of three. Give them plenty of time to work; then discuss their answers by using these discussion points:

1. Invite the youth to say which factor was highest or lowest for them.

Then have them rate the four factors again, this time asking, "On a scale from 1 to 5, how much of a role should each of the following factors play when you make a decision about whether to act with honesty and integrity?" Have the students rate each factor with a show of fingers. Which factor does your group think is most important? least important?

2, 3. Allow the youth to tell their stories if they feel comfortable doing so. Listen for common threads such as convenience or avoiding conflict in the case of doing the wrong thing, or courage or faith in the case of doing the right thing.

4. Record the students' responses on a markerboard or large sheet of paper. Ask follow-up questions for clarification if you need to do so. Challenge the youth to keep these long-term benefits in mind so that they can act with integrity in difficult situations.

Look at the Book

Ask a volunteer to read aloud **Proverbs 11:3** from *The Message* ("The integrity of the honest keeps them on track; the deviousness of crooks brings them to ruin.")

Say: "This Scripture presents two choices, and each has an outcome. On the one hand, being honest will 'keep us on track'; on the other hand, being dishonest or 'devious' will 'bring us to ruin.' "

Then ask a youth to read aloud **Job 2:1-3.**

Ask:

• How cool would it be if God singled you out and said that no one was as honest and true as you? What kind of behavior do you think Job had to display to become so highly regarded by God?

Have another youth continue the story, reading **Job 2:4-8.**

Ask:

• OK, oozing sores aren't as cool as being singled out as a person of integrity. Why, do you think, did God allow Satan to test Job?

Have yet another youth read aloud **Job 2:9-10.**

Then say: "If you're familiar with the Book of Job, you know that a lot of people gave Job bad advice. In these verses, even his wife gives him bad advice by telling him to curse God. But as the Scripture tells us, Job refused to curse God and did not sin."

Say: "This part is just the beginning of Job's story. As the story continues, the trials get harder, Job's friends tell him that he is to blame for his predicament, and Job is tempted to turn from God. But Job, despite all of the hardship, keeps his integrity."

Wrap-up

Instruct the students to write **Proverbs 11:3** in their own words. Challenge the youth to think about situations in their lives when they have had trouble doing the right thing and to use these situations as inspiration for their paraphrase of the passage. Give the youth plenty of time to work. Then invite volunteers to read aloud their version of **Proverbs 11:3.**

Close in prayer, asking God's help in living lives of integrity and staying focused on the long-term benefits of being honest.

The Call: Knowing God

The Big Idea

Our heavenly Father wants to know us and be known by us. Knowing God is not simply a matter of doing, saying, or professing the right things; rather it involves orienting our minds and hearts toward God.

Session Texts

• **Psalm 46:10:** ("Be still, and know that I am God!")

• **Jeremiah 31:33-34a** (God makes a new covenant with Israel.)

• **Matthew 7:22-23** (Jesus tells the importance of doing God's will.)

Before You Teach This Lesson

All of our acts of mercy, worship, devotion, and justice are important to our spiritual maturity. But just because we pray every morning, go to church each week, and volunteer our time to serve others doesn't mean that we know God. To truly know the Lord, we have to pray, worship, and serve with our hearts and minds set on God.

Think through these questions as you prepare to teach this session:

• How do you set your mind and heart on God when you pray or participate in worship?

• What have you learned about God's will for your life through sincere, intimate conversation with God in prayer?

• When, if ever, are you afraid to give yourself fully to God?

What You'll Need
Bibles, paper, and pens or pencils, concordances (optional)

Opener: How Well Do You Know God?

If you have more than five youth, divide the students into teams of three or four. Challenge the teams to come up with the one word or phrase that best describes who God is. Give the teams several minutes to come up with their word or phrase. Then challenge them to find Scriptures to support their choice. Provide concordances if you have them.

Allow plenty of time for the teams to work. Then invite the teams to read aloud their lists and supporting Scriptures.

Say: "While learning about God is important, there is a difference between knowing about God and really getting to know God. Getting to know God requires giving your heart and mind fully to God."

Teaching

Many older youth will know the difference between being truly devoted to something and just running through the motions. Youth who are athletes and musicians will know that if they don't take practice seriously, they won't improve. And most high school students will have discovered that staring at a book for a couple of hours doesn't pass for studying.

Explain that faith involves giving our hearts and minds fully to God. We need to be aware of when we just run through the motions or when we struggle to be faithful. We need to use discipline so that we can focus on God.

Handout: Know God

Distribute copies of the "Know God" handout, and instruct the youth to complete the worksheet. Give them plenty of time to work; then discuss the worksheet:

> **What You'll Need**
> copies of "Know God"
> worksheet (on the CD-ROM)

1. A big part of getting to know someone is conversation in which both persons truly listen to each other. Ask the youth to think about how much of this high-quality time they spend with God.

2. Invite youth to read aloud their paragraphs. What themes or attributes come up more than once? Affirm each person's unique understanding of who God is, and challenge each person to find ways to better know God.

3. Stress that the youth need to examine whether they fall into the traps of being super-religious, a brainiac, a goodie-goodie, or a name-checker and that this exercise is not an opportunity to

accuse others of falling into one or more of these traps. Explain that the best way to avoid getting stuck in these traps is to be aware of them.

4. Challenge the students to commit to making one change in the coming week that will help them better know God. Help the youth think of changes that are both effective and doable.

Look at the Book

Ask a volunteer to read aloud **Matthew 7:21-23.**

Say: "Jesus clearly says that calling ourselves his followers or even doing things in his name isn't good enough. If we truly want to know Christ, we have to do God's will."

Ask:

• How can we know whether something we do is truly God's will? *(Answers may include prayer and seeking guidance from Scripture.)*

Ask a volunteer to read aloud **Psalm 46:10.**

Ask:

• How do Scripture and personal experience assure you that you can trust God? When, if ever, do you struggle to trust God?

• How does knowing God help us face life's difficulties?

Wrap-up

Remind the youth that we are called to know our Father and that knowing God means giving our minds and hearts to the Lord. We shouldn't get so caught up in how much we know or believe or how many good things we do that we glorify ourselves instead of God.

Close in prayer, expressing a desire to get to know the Lord better and to avoid the traps that keep us from giving our hearts and minds to God.

The Call: You Are Here

The Big Idea

To use a map effectively, we must fist know where we are. Without that key piece of information, any map is useless. Likewise, to answer God's call, we must be able to identify where we are so that we can better understand where we need to go. We can map our spiritual maturity by defining four stages of development: seeker, believer, follower, and reproducer.

Session Texts

• **Matthew 28:19-20** (The Great Commission)

• **Acts 8:30-31** (Philip and the Ethiopian)

Before You Teach This Lesson

Where are you on your spiritual journey? Where have you come from? Where are you headed?

You cannot help guide your youth along the path of discipleship without traveling that path yourself. Read through this lesson and the descriptions of "seeker," "believer," "follower," and "reproducer." Think about which of these stages of the journey fits you best. Think back on when in your life have you advanced from one stage to the next. What enabled you to take that next step?

Think through these questions as you prepare to teach this lesson:

• When did your Christian journey begin? How did God lead you down the path toward Christian discipleship before you even knew that path existed?

• In what ways does God lead you (or push you) toward a more fulfilling life in Christ?

• If you had only one hour to express to your students the meaning of walking the path of Christian discipleship, what would you say?

Opener: Where Am I?

Select one volunteer, and ask this person to step out of the room for a minute. While this person is gone, have the rest of the group come up with a location for this person. The location may be a foreign country, another city, or a landmark in your community. Make sure that everyone is clear on exactly what location has been chosen.

Invite the volunteer to return to the room, and challenge this person to discover the location you've chosen by asking yes-or-no questions (such as, "Am I in this state?" and "Am I north of the equator?"). Allow the person to ask up to twenty questions before revealing the location. Repeat this game with other youth as time allows.

Say: "The Christian faith is a journey. As Christians, we need to think about where we are on our journey and where we are going."

Ask:

• Where does our journey as Christians start? *(Answers may include at baptism, when one makes a profession of faith, when one first learns about Christ, or before one is born.)*

• If we think of our faith as a journey, where will our faith lead us?

Teaching

This session looks at the Christian journey in four stages: seeker, believer, follower, and reproducer. These stages aren't biblical or scientific, and not everyone will be able to identify exact instances when they go from one stage to the next. Thinking of our faith journey as a continuum instead of a series of stages may help older youth. You might also point out that this continuum doesn't have a definite starting point or endpoint. The journey began long before we were born, and we will not complete the journey in our lifetime.

Handout: On the Journey

What You'll Need
copies of "On the Journey"
handout (on the CD-ROM)

Distribute copies of "On the Journey,"
and instruct the youth to complete it. Give
them plenty of time to work.

Then discuss their answers by using these discussion points:

1. Some youth may have been born into a family in which going to
church and teaching children about the faith are important. Others
may have been introduced to Christ by a friend. Still, others may
have had an extraordinary experience that made them aware of
God's presence. Mission trips, weeks at church camp, and other
"mountaintop experiences" often help young people take another
step along their journey and put their faith into perspective. Assure
the youth that we all come to faith and grow in faith in unique
ways.

2. Do not pressure the youth to talk about where they think they are
right now. Explain that regardless of where someone is on his or
her spiritual journey, we can all grow as Christians. Reproducers
are by no means finished with the journey. Also assure the students
that the Christian journey is often gradual—few, if any, Christians
go from being a seeker to being a reproducer overnight.

3. Important ways to keep moving along in our journeys include
prayer, worship, Scripture reading and study, fellowship and
Christian community, the love of other Christians, and serving and
showing Christ's love to others. Emphasize the importance of
participation in a loving and supportive Christian community.

4. Challenge the youth to get specific. Can they make daily habits out
of prayer and Bible study? If youth are trying to grow into
reproducers, can they think of situations where they aren't
comfortable discussing their faith and think of ways to work
through that discomfort?

Look at the Book

Ask volunteers to read aloud **Acts 8:26-37,** with each person reading
two or three verses.

Ask:

- Who's the seeker in this story? *(the Ethiopian)*

- Who is the reproducer? *(Philip)*

- How does Philip help the Ethiopian go from being a seeker to being a believer? *(by allowing the Holy Spirit to work within him, by studying the Scripture with the Ethiopian, and by telling the extraordinary story of Jesus)*

- How, do you think, did Philip grow spiritually as a result of this experience?

Say: "In this story the Ethiopian becomes a believer and is baptized into the church. But Scripture is clear that belief is not the end of the journey. We need to live out our belief and become disciples of Christ."

Ask a volunteer to read aloud **Matthew 28:19-20.**

Say: "This Scripture is often known as the Great Commission. Jesus commissioned his disciples to tell the world about how Christ had died for the sins of the world and risen from the dead. In other words, he asked his closest followers to become reproducers."

Instruct the youth to think of three ways they can follow Jesus' instructions to "Go . . . and make disciples of all nations" and to write these ways on the back of their handout. Examples may include talking to friends about their faith, setting an example by obeying Christ's teaching, and showing people the joy that comes with knowing that God loves us. Encourage the youth to be creative and to think of things that fit their gifts and personalities.

Wrap-up

Remind the youth that the Christian journey does not end in this life. No matter where they are, they can always go further. Ask them to take home their handout as a reminder of where they are and what they can do to take the next step.

Close in prayer, asking God's guidance as we all continue along our lifelong journey of faith.

The Call: Can You Hear Me Now?

The Big Idea

Even the most devout, faithful Christians go through times when God seems distant and prayers seem to go unanswered. But God is always present, even in the most dire circumstances. Through worship, we become more aware of how God's Holy Spirit is at work in our lives.

Session Texts

• **Numbers 14:1-3** (The Israelites complain to Moses and Aaron.)

• **Deuteronomy 8:10-14** (Do not forget the Lord your God.)

• **John 4:23** (The true worshipers will worship in spirit and truth.)

Before You Teach This Lesson

How do you worship, thank, and praise God? Do you say prayers of thanksgiving before meals, or at times when you especially sense God's presence? Do you give glory to God when you do the things you love (whether they be sports, music, enjoying nature, or something else)?

Think through these questions as you prepare to teach this lesson:

• How does your congregation worship? What elements of worship appeal most to you?

• What about God's love most compels you to respond in worship?

• For what do you thank God? How do you express your thanks?

• If you had only one hour to express to your students how to respond to God's call through worship, what would you say?

Opener: Can You Hear Me Now?

What You'll Need
at least one set of short-range walkie-talkies

Obtain pairs of inexpensive walkie-talkies. You can get a new set of toy walkie-talkies for about $10 at most toy stores, but check with parents in your congregation to see whether they have old sets that their kids don't use anymore.

Hand out the pairs of walkie-talkies to pairs of youth, and tell the students to walk around the church building and see how far apart they can go before they lose their signal. Repeat the activity so that all of the youth have a chance to participate. Find out which set of walkie-talkies has the longest range or which pair of youth is able to get a clear signal from the greatest distance.

Ask:

• What other factors affected your reception? (Answers may include interference from other walkie-talkies and wireless devices, and the battery power in the walkie-talkies.)

Say: "Sometimes, talking to God is like talking on these walkie-talkies. We struggle to hear God, and we wonder whether God can hear us."

Teaching

God always hears our prayers, but sometimes we feel like the Lord isn't paying attention. On the other hand, God calls out to us, and sometimes we don't pay attention. Like kids with walkie-talkies, we often struggle to get a clear signal when we we're communicating with God.

One important way we find a clear signal is worship, where we can say to God, "Can you hear me now?" Worship keeps despair, frustration, and fear from overwhelming us.

What You'll Need
copies of the "Worship Connection" worksheet (on the CD-ROM)

Handout: Worship Connection

Hand out copies of "Worship Connection," and have the youth complete it in pairs or groups of three. Allow time for work; then discuss their answers:

1. Allow volunteers to tell and explain some of their answers. Do the situations that make the youth feel close to God have anything in common? What about the situations in which God feels distant?

2. Explain to the youth that various ways of worship exist. The Holy Spirit moves people to worship God in unique ways. Ask the youth whether any elements of worship not listed draw them closer to God.

3. A Christian can worship on a skateboard, while hiking in the woods, or by playing a song. Note that worship often involves Christians coming together to glorify God.

4. Answers may include inspiration, courage to face the week ahead, peace, or the love and support of a Christian community. Worship refreshes our spirits and helps us focus on what is truly important.

Look at the Book

Ask a volunteer to read aloud **Deuteronomy 8:10-14.**

Say: "Human beings have an arrogant tendency to take the credit when things are going well and none of the blame when times are tough. Worship helps us remember that God is in charge and that God is good. In worship, we give thanks for God's blessings, we confess our sins, and we ask for God's help and guidance."

Ask:

• Think about worship with your congregation. What parts of the worship service are focused on praise and thanksgiving?

• What parts of the service are focused on confessing our sins?

• What parts are focused on asking God for help and guidance?

Wrap-up

Ask a volunteer to read aloud **John 4:23.**

Say, "God wants us to worship; and in worship, we hear God more clearly."

Encourage the students to pay close attention to the next worship service they attend. What parts of the service do they find especially powerful? How does the worship experience bring them closer to God?

Close in prayer, thanking the Creator for the opportunity to worship and asking for God's patience when we fail to hear God's voice.

The Call: Keeping the Lines Clear

The Big Idea

The realm of communication has four major players: the sender, the receiver, the message, and the noise. In our conversations with God, we need to eliminate the noise so that we can accurately and consistently hear God's voice.

Session Texts

• **1 Samuel 3:8-10** (God calls Samuel.)

• **1 Kings 19:11-13** (Elijah hears God's still, small voice.)

• **Isaiah 30:21b** ("Your ears shall hear a word behind you, saying, 'This is the way; walk in it.")

Before You Teach This Lesson

Think about what God has called you to do in your life. When have you eagerly responded to God's call? When have you run away from it? When have you had trouble figuring out what God was saying to you?

Listening to the Lord can be difficult, especially if we don't make prayer a habit. We are inundated with noise that makes focusing on God's voice a challenge. Noise may come in the form of pride, greed, or stress. To grow in our relationship with the God, we need to find ways to shut out the noise and keep the lines clear.

Think about these questions as you prepare to teach this lesson:

• When you pray, how much difficulty do you have focusing on God? What "noise" distracts you when you pray?

• What interests or obsessions distract you from your bond with God? How do they keep you from fully obeying God's will for your life?

• How much effort do you put into listening to God? What practices help you focus on God's voice?

• If you had only one hour to teach your students about blocking out the noise and focusing on God's voice, what would you say?

Opener: Make Some Noise

What You'll Need
noise makers, markerboard or large sheet of paper, markers, timer, one or more index cards

Beforehand, write on an index card a set of five to ten instructions for drawing. You might write, for example, "Draw a rectangle. On either side of the rectangle, draw a small circle. Place a dot on the edge of each circle so that each dot is as far away from the rectangle as possible. Connect the dots with a line that goes through both circles and the rectangle."

Select two volunteers, one to give the instructions on the card and one to follow them by drawing on a markerboard or large sheet of paper. Place these persons at opposite ends of the room. The rest of the youth will distract the two volunteers to keep them from completing their task. Give noisemakers to the distracters. Give the two volunteers exactly one minute to read and follow the instructions.

After one minute, ask the person who gave instructions:

• In what ways did you try to overcome all of the noise so that your partner could hear your instructions?

Ask the persons who tried to follow the instructions:

• How did you try to focus on the instructions being given to you?

Ask everyone:

• What distracts you from the instructions that God gives you?

Teaching

Youth today have grown up in a world where multitasking is commonplace. Our computers and phones enable us to do several things at once. A person today might chat on the phone with one person while typing instant messages to another, all the while keeping an eye on the score of a football game, listening to music, and downloading software.

While doing several things at once may be easy, doing any one of these things well can be difficult.

The Call: Keeping the Lines Clear   43

As Christians, we need to clear our minds, hearts, and schedules for God. For older youth, doing so can be especially difficult. High school provides endless opportunities to try new things, develop talents, and get involved in the school and the community. A driver's license opens up even more opportunities. Add to these things the stress that comes with keeping grades up, forming one's identity, managing relationships with friends, and planning for the future, and you get a lot of "noise" that makes actively listening to God challenging.

Older youth need help identifying and blocking out this "noise" and focusing on communicating with God.

Handout: Keep It Down!

> **What You'll Need**
> copies of "Keep It Down!" (on the CD-ROM)

Hand out copies of "Keep It Down!" and instruct the youth to complete the worksheet in pairs or groups of three. Give them plenty of time to work.

Then discuss their answers by using these discussion points:

1. Don't be judgmental. Assure the youth that many adults, even longtime devoted Christians, struggle to focus when they pray. Also explain to the youth that God speaks to us even when we aren't praying. God may send us a message through another person, an event, or a sudden feeling that we have. We just need to pay attention so that we know when God is calling out to us.

2. Be clear that some of the items listed are not necessarily bad. For instance, playing a sport or an instrument is a good thing. But if we get so obsessed about our performance that we can't focus on anything else, it becomes a problem.

3. This question ties in to the "Hanging Out With God" and "Prayer" sessions from the "Glow" unit, so the students may have thought about it already.

4. Consider having the students write their prayer commitments on a slip of paper that they can keep in their wallet or purse.

Look at the Book

Ask a volunteer to read aloud **1 Kings 19:11-13.**

Say: "This passage illustrates the importance of eliminating the noises that distract us from God. In this Scripture, the prophet Elijah is on the run from the evil queen Jezebel, who wants to kill him; and he eagerly awaits instructions from God. As Elijah listens for God, he witnesses a mighty wind, an earthquake, and a fire. But God doesn't speak through any of these natural wonders. Instead, God speaks in a whisper in the silence."

Ask:

• How do you expect to hear (or experience) God's voice?

Ask volunteers to read aloud the following Scriptures as a survey of some of the ways God speaks to us:

- **Numbers 22:22-35**
- **Daniel 5:5-9, 17-28**
- **Luke 1:26-37**
- **Acts 9:1-9**

Say: "Sometimes God speaks to us in obvious ways; sometimes God speaks quietly. But in either case, we are most likely to hear the Lord clearly when we focus on God's voice."

Ask:

• Based on what we've talked about today, what are some ways you can get rid of the noise in your life and focus on God's voice?

Wrap-up

Read aloud **1 Samuel 3:1-10.**

Say: "Samuel doesn't recognize God's voice right away, but God keeps speaking to him. the Lord is patient and persistent; but ultimately, God wants us to listen."

Close in prayer, asking the Lord to help your youth shut out distractions and listen carefully for God's voice.

The Call: Called to Follow

The Big Idea

Christ is calling us to follow him. This commitment involves risking everything. It means that our life is no longer our own. Christ has commissioned us to a life of ministry in which everything we do is directed toward God's mission on earth.

Session Texts

• **Matthew 28:16-20** (The Great Commission)

• **Luke 9:57-62** (Jesus explains the cost of discipleship.)

Before You Teach This Lesson

Following Christ is not meant to be easy or comfortable. Often, living out our faith involves courage, sacrifice, and a willingness to set aside our own interests. Jesus was up front with his followers about what discipleship required: Giving our whole lives over to Christ and never looking back.

Dropping everything and responding to God's call can be difficult in a culture where numerous things compete for our time and attention. God asks us to give ourselves fully to following Christ, and God doesn't want excuses. What do you need to do to commit more fully to a life of discipleship?

Read **Luke 9:57-62** and **Matthew 28:16-20,** and reflect on the following questions:

• What earthly commitments keep you from giving yourself fully to Christ?

• How do you respond to the Great Commission? (A more traditional reading is, "Go therefore and make disciples of all nations, baptizing them in the name of the Father and of the Son and of the Holy Spirit, and teaching them to obey everything that I have commanded you.")

• How can you challenge and equip your youth to "go therefore and make disciples"?

Opener: Dance As I Dance

What You'll Need
empty space for dancing;
optional: dance music (with
appropriate lyrics)

Select a teen to be the leader. Clear out a large, empty space so that every youth has room to dance. The leader will perform a series of dance moves. Everyone else will attempt to copy the moves. Disqualify anyone unable to follow the leader. Play until one participant, other than the leader, remains.

Repeat this game, each time with a different leader. Then ask:

• Who are some of the leaders you follow?

• What risks and challenges come with following these persons?

Say: "In this game, following the leader may have involved embarrassing yourself a little. But the cost of following Christ can be much greater. On the other hand, the rewards are much greater."

Handout: Followers

What You'll Need
copies of "Followers" (on
the CD-ROM)

Hand out copies of "Followers," and instruct the youth to complete it. Give them plenty of time to work; then discuss their answers by using these discussion points:

1. Allow the youth to name some of the people whom they follow. Which persons (or occupations such as teacher or pastor) came up most often? Which were unique to one student? How much influence do friends and peers have over your students?

2. This question is for personal reflection and assessment. Do not pressure the youth to talk about their answers.

3. Record the students' answers on a markerboard or large sheet of paper. Which words came up most often? Which were unique to one student? Invite the youth to explain the words they chose.

4. Explain to the teens that Jesus isn't necessarily asking them to give up all of their possessions and friends, but that we sometimes have to put our faith ahead of other things that we hold dear. These situations may be painful, but we can trust God to see us through.

Look at the Book

Ask a volunteer to read aloud **Luke 9:57-62.**

Say: "Many of the people who witnessed Jesus wanted to become his followers. In this Scripture, Jesus explains to these people that following him is not about comfort and security."

Ask:

• What makes following Jesus difficult or uncomfortable for you?

• Why, do you think, is following Jesus so urgent? Why does Jesus ask people to follow him *right now*?

• How might people have reacted when Jesus told them to skip a parent's funeral or not to say goodbye to friends and family? How, do you think, would you have reacted if Jesus had said these things to you?

• What have you given up to follow Christ? What else can you give up?

Say: "Christ asks people to sacrifice various things. Not all of us will have to leave behind friends and families. But we all need to be willing to give up money, possessions, and certain behaviors and devote ourselves more fully to Christ."

Wrap-up

Encourage the youth in the coming week to think seriously about what they absolutely need and what they could give up if Jesus asked them to forfeit certain things. Challenge the students to find ways they can give more of their time, talents, and money to Christ and his work on earth.

Close in prayer, asking God for the courage and conviction to be true followers of Jesus Christ.

CD-ROM System Requirements
• 64 MB RAM Adobe® Acrobat™ Reader, version 4.0 or higher
• Flash 7 or higher
• Web browser
